The Only Galaxy Note 4 Guide That You Will Ever Need

AMARPREET SINGH

THE THOUGHT FLAME
TURNING SPARK INTO FLAME

info@thethoughtflame.com

www.thethoughtflame.com

Table of Contents

Introduction

This book contains proven steps and strategies on how to use the Galaxy Note 4 as well as is designed for those who want to get the most of their Samsung device, regardless of their Android experience.

In this book you will learn a variety of things ranging from how to do basic things with your phone such as turning it on or off to more complex things like troubleshooting annoying issues that may arise with the phone. Regardless of your experience with Android devices, I promise that by the end of this book you will be an expert at handling not only the Galaxy Note 4, but practically any Android phone that you will get your hands on.

Thanks again for downloading this book and I really hope that you enjoy it!

Chapter 1: The Basics of The Galaxy Note 4

While the Galaxy Note 4 may look like your average smartphone, it is more advanced than even you may be aware. In this chapter I want to teach you about the basic look of your phone and go into detail about every part of it, so you can understand how to do basic things with it such as shut it on or off or how to even use the camera correctly.

The Basic Layout of Your Phone

Every Galaxy Note 4 has a total of 6 different buttons on the phone itself: 2 of which are hard buttons that you can press and 4 of which of considered to be soft buttons (touch screen capable)

The Soft Keys

The soft keys do not need to be pressed. Touch each button lightly to perform one of the following actions:

The Menu Key-Displays the context-based menu. For instance, at the Home screen, the Main menu is shown. In the Gmail application, "Compose", "Search", and other options are shown.

The Home Key-Displays the Home screen at any time.

The Back Key-Returns the Galaxy Note to the previous screen or menu.

The Search Key-Displays the context-based search. At the Home screen or in the web browser, this button automatically opens Google search. In applications like Gmail, this button opens the Mail Search field.

The Hard Keys

Volume Control-Controls the volume of the earpiece, speakerphone, and media. Press the Volume Up button to increase the volume or press the Volume Down button to decrease it.

Power Button-Turns the Galaxy Note on and off. Locks and unlocks the phone.

How To Turn Your Galaxy Note 4 On and Off

To turn the Galaxy Note on, press the Power button and immediately release it. The phone starts up. To turn the Galaxy Note off, press and hold the Power button until the Phone Options window appears. Once done a dialog box should appear next. Touch the OK prompt and the phone will shut down automatically.

How To Navigate The Home Screen of Your Phone

There are many ways to navigate the screens of the Galaxy Note. Use the following tips while exploring the phone:

1. Touch the arrow key to return to the Home screen at any time. Any application or tool that is currently in use will be in the same state when it is re-opened.

2. Touch the arrow key at any time to return to the previous screen.

Touch the top of the screen and move your finger down to show running programs. Use the S Pen instead of the back button and the key with two lines surrounded by a small box.

The Different Types of Objects on The Home Screen

Each home screen on the Galaxy Note is fully customizable. Each screen can hold one or more of the following items:

1. A Widget-A tool that can be used directly on the Home screen without opening like an application. Widgets usually take up the whole screen or a fraction of it while applications are added as icons. The Weather widget is shown in Figure 8.

2. An Application-A program that opens in a new window, such as Gmail or a game. Applications are added to the Home screen as icons.

3. A Shortcut-A shortcut to just about anything on your phone. Make a shortcut to a Settings screen, a direct dial for a single person, or a set of directions for a specific location.

4. A Folder-A folder of application icons or shortcuts. Please note that a folder cannot store widgets. To add an object to a folder, touch and hold the object and drag it over the folder.

How To Organize The Objects On Your Home Screen

Customize the Home screens by adding, deleting, or moving around objects. To add an object to a Home screen:

1. Touch the menu key. Once the main menu appears touch the plus sign icon. The Add to Home menu should appear. Once it does touch a type of object. A list of objects appears. Then touch an object in the list. The object is added to the Home screen that you are currently viewing.

Please be aware that if you try to add an object to a Home screen that is already full, it will automatically be added to the next screen that has available space.

To delete an object, touch and hold the object until the phone briefly vibrates and the small garbage can icon appears at the bottom of the page. Move the object over garbage can icon located at the bottom of the screen and release the screen. The object is removed from the Home screen.

Managing Your Contacts On Your Phone

On the Galaxy Note, a contact can be added to the Phonebook on the device, to the Phonebook linked to Google or another account, or to the SIM card. Adding a contact to a Google or to another account allows total syncing of contacts across your phone and online account, easily backing up your contacts.

To add a new contact:

1. Touch the phone icon at the bottom of the screen until the keypad appears.

2. Enter the phone number of the contact you wish to add and touch Add to Contacts until the Add to Contacts dialog appears.

3. Touch Create contact. The Save Location window should appear and then touch Phone if you wish to save the contact directly to your phone memory. Touch SIM if you wish to save the contact to your SIM card. If you touch 'SIM', the contact will be backed up on your SIM card in case anything happens to your phone. However, a SIM card contact can only store the name, a single phone number, and a single email address. You can also touch the name of an account, if you wish to back up your contacts online in case your phone is lost or broken. The SIM Contact Information screen appears, or the Full Contact Information screen

appears, depending on your selection.

4. Touch a field to edit it. The information is entered.

5. Touch the back key at any time to hide the keyboard.

6. Touch the Save button. The contact is saved and the keypad appears.

To update an existing contact:

1. Instead of the create contact button you will want to press the Update existing contact button.

2. Touch the name of a contact. The Contact Information screen should appear, and the new number is automatically added.

3. Touch the Save button and the contact information will be updated automatically.

To Find An Existing Contact

After adding new contacts to your phone's Phonebook, eventually there will be a time where you will need to look up a certain person's information. To find stored contact information:

1. Touch the person icon until the Phonebook appears.

2. Touch the magnifying glass key while viewing the Phonebook to search for a contact.

3.Type the partial or full name of a contact. The matching results appear or touch and hold the alphabet on the right side of the screen. Then move your finger up or down while holding the screen to scroll through the alphabet.

4. Touch the double arrow icon located at the top of the screen. The most recently contacted numbers will then appear shortly.

Chapter 2: What Makes The Galaxy Note 4 So Special?

Like all the previous models, Galaxy Note 4 comes with major hardware and physical upgrades, and has certainly upped the ante. Let's look into the new features and upgrades it brings:

The Awesome Fingerprint Scanner

The upgraded fingerprint scanner effectively ensures the safety of the users' data. It is divided into two parts, one is on the home button while the other is incorporated into the screen; the device will make use of both the scanners for identification and security purposes.

Brand New Ultraviolet Sensor

The Galaxy Note 4 includes the world's first ultraviolet sensor in a mobile phone, enabling it to detect the strength of the ultraviolet rays from the sun. It also includes pedometer and a heart rate sensor that will keep track of your fitness and health. Although Samsung does not want the Galaxy Note 4 to be seen as a medical device, it has added a lot of sensors and features that make it an excellent health tracking device, as well as a potential medical device.

Improved Battery

Gone are the days when phones were so battery efficient that you could go on without charging your phone for days. While the batteries have gotten better, so have the phones, and now our phones use a lot more battery now than they have ever before. Frankly speaking, it is not surprising at all if you have to charge your phone daily. The amazing, fast, beautiful, and detailed applications that we have today require a lot of battery power as well. Samsung has tackled this problem in a new way with the

Galaxy Note 4. Not only does it feature a battery with a higher capacity, but the charging times have been dramatically reduced. Unlike any other phone, the Galaxy Note 4 charges at one of the fastest speeds than any other phone on the market and can even reach 50% charge from 0% in just under 30 minutes.

Multitasking Capability

The Note 4 comes with a new multitasking interface. It includes TouchWiz Nature UX 3.0 custom skin. With some very simple gestures, you can use more than one application at the same time. You can split the screen in two to use 2 applications at the same time, or you can shrink one application so it hovers over another and   still have the ability to use them both.

Photo Note Feature

This is another great feature introduced by Samsung. It allows you to take photos of existing notes and convert them from analog to digital format. You can convert notes, change colors, and then modify or edit them, as you need. It comes in handy when you want to modify some existing notes, like assignments or lectures, as it allows you to edit and add to the existing notes.

Better Camera

While camera upgrades in smartphones are not that big of a news, the features that are added to them can take the spotlight. This time, Samsung has solved a huge problem with the 16 MP camera in Note 4, allowing the users to take good quality photos even in dark surroundings. Its Smart Optical Image Stabilizer (OIS) increases the time of exposure when lighting is low/ poor and also prevents the camera shake. The front facing camera also uses better angles and helps you take better selfies. Samsung has focused on selfies a lot and introduced various camera modes, as well as added features, which make taking selfies really very convenient. For instance, when you use the front camera, the beauty mode on the phone is activated automatically, so you never have to worry about activating it yourself.

High Quality Screen

While the size of the screen has remained unchanged, the screen of Galaxy Note 4 has been upgraded. The Quad HD Super AMOLED Display with a pixel density of 515 ppi further enhances the already amazing viewing experience by producing crystal clear and vivid images. It is virtually impossible to see pixels on your phone with this screen. Even if you put the phone right in front of your eye, you will not be able to notice any pixels. The screen is simply stunning! When compared to an iPhone 6 or iPhone 6 +, Galaxy Note 4 takes the lead with a superior screen.

The Advanced S-Pen

The advanced S-Pen with enhanced pressure sensitivity improves the handwriting experience even further. The pen has a natural brush effect that emulates writing on paper with a calligraphy/ fountain pen, and the handwriting features have been incorporated into many different apps along with the Air Command functionality, including Screen Write, Smart Select, Image Clip, and Action Memo.

Enhanced SD Card

The Galaxy Note 4 gives you more liberty in terms of capacity and storage space. It can easily handle an SD card of up to 128 GB. When combined with its internal memory, you can have more than 150 GB of storage space.

Chapter 3: How To Use All Of Your Phone's Awesome Software Features

Unlike other phones, the Galaxy Note 4 comes loaded with a variety of different types of software that you can use on a daily basis. Whether you use the Stay Smart feature or want to use the UV Light sensor, there are endless things that you can do with this phone.

This chapter is solely dedicated to teaching you how to use all of these awesome software features so that you can have more fun with your phone instead of countless headaches.

The Smart Stay Feature

The Galaxy Note 4 comes with the Smart Stay feature. Although it is not enabled by default, you can enable it easily from the settings. When you enable it, it uses the front camera to detect whether or not you are looking at the screen. The screen remains on as long as you are looking at it, and dims/ turns off when you look away. This makes the phone more battery efficient. The face detection has also been improved so even when your face is off-axis, it is able to detect it.

The Adaptive Display Feature

The software has been tweaked to make the most of the Quad HD Super AMOLED Display. The adaptive display feature is turned on by default and slightly adjusts the screen depending on the content you are viewing. Though the screen already makes everything look better, this display mode further enhances the color and the clarity of whatever it is that you are viewing.

The Ultra Power Saving Mode

To fully understand the power of the Ultra

Power Saving Mode, you need to understand the Power Saving Mode to see how it differs from it. When you enable the Power Saving Mode to save battery, the brightness of the phone is automatically reduced, as it is one of the most power consuming things. The clock speed of the phone's Central Processing Unit is clamped down while the background processes like syncing are also disabled. With this mode, the functionality of the phone is not compromised and the battery consumption is greatly reduced.

Now, the Ultra Power Saving Mode! With this mode your phone can run for 24 hours and only use 10% of the battery, so you can make your phone last for about 10 days without having to recharge it. This mode takes some aggressive measures to save as much of the battery as possible, and even compromises the functionality of the phone. When this mode is turned on, the brilliant screen of the Note 4 turns grey and the home screen changes to a very basic theme. The access to the apps is also limited, like Memo, Internet browser, Calculator, Messages, Voice Recorder, etc. But this mode is customizable and supports some popular third party apps, so if you want you can enable WhatsApp, Facebook, etc. in it. The apps running in the background are closed and some cores of the powerful CPU are also turned off, while others are down-clocked to a mere 1.5 GHz. The cellular data network for Internet, Bluetooth, and Wi-Fi are also turned off, while others are down-clocked to a mere 1.5 GHz. The cellular data network for Internet, Bluetooth, and Wi-Fi are also turned off and only start working when the screen is turned on.

Although this pretty much turns your smartphone into a dumb phone, given that it can make your phone last for a day with only 10% battery, it can be remarkably useful. It can be turned on from the Settings menu in the   Power Saving Section.

The One Handed Mode

Unlike other phones, what makes this phone really stand out is that the Galaxy Note 4 is a tablet. While the tablets are more functional and useful than the smartphones, the additional screen size can also make them difficult to use, especially with one hand. Most of the phone users like to multitask, using the phone with one hand and doing something else with the other. It is usually difficult to do both at the same time when you have a tablet, but Samsung has taken care of that problem in the Note 4 with the One Handed Mode.

When the One Handed Mode is enabled, you have to drag your thumb from the edge of the phone to the centre of the screen, and the phone will automatically shrink the screen size to make the phone convenient to use. The size of the keyboard also shrinks so that you can type easily. This mode is highly customizable and you can adjust it to your needs by using options like One Handed Input, etc.

The Pop Up Apps Feature

The Note 4 has taken multitasking to a new level. A new feature called 'Pop Up Apps' allows you to use up to 5 apps at the same time, in addition to the main app running in the background. The apps that are popped up can be resized and used simultaneously with all the other apps. You can zoom in and out of those apps seamlessly, so, in essence, it allows you to multitask by using 6 apps at the same time. It may sound like so many apps will crowd the screen, but given Note 4' s large screen size, it will be no problem   whatsoever.

With the endless amount of features that are present on this phone, you should have no problem finding multiple uses for it. With all of these different features I would be surprised if you didn't fall in love with this phone immediately.

Chapter 4: Some Helpful Tips and Tricks To Bringing Out The Best In Your Galaxy Note 4

Just as with any other smart phone, there are a few tips and tricks that you can utilize to help bring out the most in your phone. This chapter is solely dedicated to helping you bring out the best that your phone has to offer so that you can enjoy your phone for as long as you have it.

Maximizing The Life of Your Battery

There are numerous things that you can do to help bring out the most of your cellphone battery on the Galaxy Note 4. Some of these things include:

1. Lock the phone whenever it is not in use. To lock the phone, press and release the Power button.

2. Keep the Screen Timeout feature set to a small amount of time, which will dim and turn off the screen when the phone is idle.

3. Turn down the brightness and turn on Auto-Brightness.

4. Turn on Airplane mode when Wireless is not needed. In an area where there is little or no signal, the Galaxy Note will continually search for service, significantly draining the battery.

5. Turn off Wi-Fi and Bluetooth when the features are not in use.

6. Turn off screen animations.

7. Minimize your use of the internet.

8. Avoid using the camera and do not use the camera flash, when possible.

Freeing Up Some Memory

There are several ways to free up memory on the Galaxy Note 4. Try one of the following:

1. Uninstall applications that are no longer needed.

2. Remove all temporary internet files. To delete these files:

-Touch the world icon until the Web browser opens.

-Touch the menu key until the Browser menu appears.

-Touch Settings until the Internet Browser settings appear.

-Touch Clear all cookie data, Clear cache, or Clear history. A confirmation dialog should then appear.

-Touch the OK button and then the

corresponding data will be cleared automatically.

Capturing A Screenshot On Your Phone

You can capture pictures of the Galaxy Note's screen. To capture a screenshot, press and hold the Shift button on the S Pen. Touch and hold the screen using the S Pen. The screen momentarily flashes and a screenshot is captured. The screenshot is stored in the 'Screen Capture' folder in the Gallery.

How To View Open Windows In Your Browser Quickly

While using the Web browser, you can quickly view the open browser windows without opening the Browser menu. Touch the screen with two fingers and move them together until the website is completely zoomed out. Touch the screen with two fingers and move them together again. The open browser windows appear.

Changing The Brightness Quickly

The Galaxy Note allows you to change the brightness of the screen without opening any menus. First, you must make sure that Automatic Brightness is turned off. Once Automatic Brightness is turned off, touch and hold the Status bar at the top of the screen (the bar that contains the signal strength, time, etc.). Slide your finger to the left to decrease the brightness or to the right to increase it.

Delete A Voicemail Without Having To Listening To It

To delete a voicemail without listening to the whole thing, just press 7 while listening to it.

The voicemail is deleted and the next message starts to play.

How To Fix Problems By Troubleshooting

What To Do If Your Phone Does Not Want To Turn On

If the Galaxy Note does not turn on, try one of the following:

1. Recharge Your Battery-Use the included wall charger to charge the battery. If the battery power is extremely low, the screen will not turn on for several minutes. Do NOT use the USB port on your computer to charge the Galaxy Note, as it will not properly charge the battery.

2. Replace the battery-If you purchased the Galaxy Note a long time ago and have charged and discharged the battery about 300-400 times, you may need to replace the battery. In this case, the phone may still turn on, but the battery will die quickly.

3. Clean the battery terminals-Take out the battery and clean the gold battery contacts with a clean, dry cloth. Put the battery back in and try charging it again.

What To Do If Your Phone Is Not Responding

If the Galaxy Note is frozen or is not responding, try one of the following:

1. Restart the Galaxy Note-If the phone freezes while running an application, try holding down the Power button for 10 to 15 seconds, until the phone restarts.

2. Take the battery out-Take out the battery, wait for ten seconds, and put it back in. Turn the phone on.

3. Remove Some Media Files-Some downloaded applications or music may freeze your phone. Once you restart it try to remove some files.

__Conclusion__

Thank you again for downloading this book!

I hope this book was able to help you to learn all that there is to know about the Galaxy Note 4 and a few helpful tricks to help bring out the most that your new phone has to offer.

So, what is next for you? The next step now is for you to fully set up your Galaxy Note 4 and begin using it on a daily basis by exploring all of its incredible features. If you have read this book in its entirety, I have no doubt in my mind that you will be an expert in using your Galaxy Note 4.

About Us

The Thought Flame is committed to add value to its customers through various books, online courses and other resources. You can learn more about us and our books at www.thethoughtflame.com.

Don't forget to check out our amazing **online video courses** at www.thethoughtflame.com/courses/ to take your knowledge to another level.

To check out our **extraordinary collection of diet/cookbooks**, visit http://www.thethoughtflame.com/category/non-fictional/cookbooks/ .

As a part of our valued relationship with our customers, we keep providing you free promotional books, courses and other stuff on subscribing with us on our site. We have a strict anti-spam policy and assure you no spam mails will be sent to your mailbox.

To subscribe with us, visit www.thethoughtflame.com.

Like our work and would like to say thanks? Buy us a cup of coffee at www.thethoughtflame.com/coffee/

Author

Amarpreet Singh is an avid learner and his passion for education has made him travel, work and study all across the world. He holds three masters degrees, including MBA, from top universities in Asia.

He is author of dozens of books, many of which are Amazon's bestseller, varying in various topics and categories. He also teaches many online courses having thousands of students across the world.

He has a keen interest in international affairs, economics, global poverty and politics, financial markets and entrepreneurship, and strives to be part of a community that shares the same passion.

He has worked as consultant with organizations like Airbus and The World Bank.

He loves travelling and learning about new cultures, and has been fortunate to live/work/travel/study in countries like India, China, Korea, US, South Africa, Japan, Philippines, Singapore, Canada etc., and learn about the culture and lifestyle in each of them.

To check out more of his work, visit

www.thethoughtflame.com